FAVORITES

Unique, Distinctive Piano Arrangements of 20 Hit Songs

T0071270

Disney Characters and Artwork TM & © 2019 Disney

Disney/Pixar Elements TM & © 2019 Disney/Pixar
All Rights Reserved

ISBN 978-1-5400-3529-5

Visit Hal Leonard Online at
www.halleonard.com

Contact us:
Hal Leonard
7777 West Bluemound Road
Milwaukee, WI 53213
Email: info@halleonard.com

In Europe, contact:
Hal Leonard Europe Limited
42 Wigmore Street
Marylebone, London, W1U 2RN
Email: info@halleonardeurope.com

In Australia, contact:
Hal Leonard Australia Pty. Ltd.
4 Lentara Court
Cheltenham, Victoria, 3192 Australia
Email: info@halleonard.com.au

CONTENTS

BEAUTY AND THE BEAST
from BEAUTY AND THE BEAST

Music by ALAN MENKEN
Lyrics by HOWARD ASHMAN

Moderately, in 2

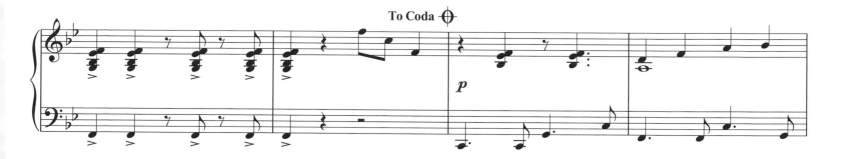

To Coda ⊕

D.S. al Coda

CODA

BELLE
from BEAUTY AND THE BEAST

Music by ALAN MENKEN
Lyrics by HOWARD ASHMAN

With motion

Moderately

To Coda ⊕ | 1.

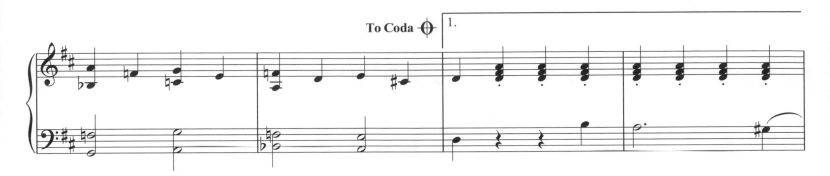

2.

D.S. al Coda

CODA

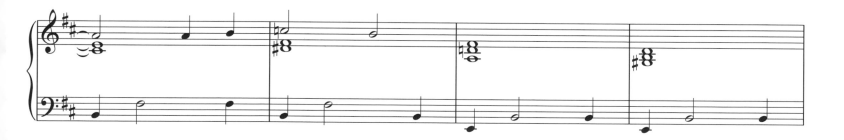

BIBBIDI-BOBBIDI-BOO
(The Magic Song)
from CINDERELLA

Words by JERRY LIVINGSTON
Music by MACK DAVID and AL HOFFMAN

CAN YOU FEEL THE LOVE TONIGHT

from THE LION KING

Music by ELTON JOHN
Lyrics by TIM RICE

CHIM CHIM CHER-EE

from MARY POPPINS

Words and Music by RICHARD M. SHERMAN
and ROBERT B. SHERMAN

Lightly, in 1

With pedal

CIRCLE OF LIFE
from THE LION KING

Music by ELTON JOHN
Lyrics by TIM RICE

Moderately

EVERMORE
from BEAUTY AND THE BEAST

Music by ALAN MENKEN
Lyrics by TIM RICE

Evenly, mysteriously

Lots of pedal throughout

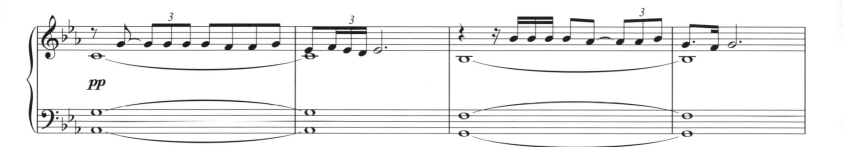

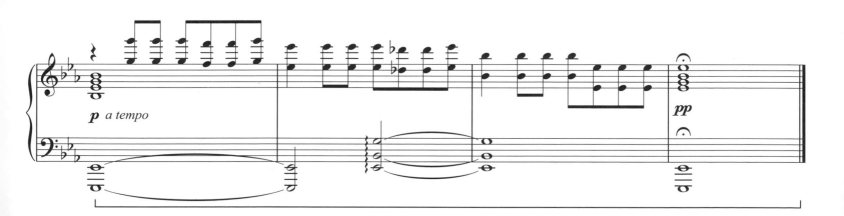

FOR THE FIRST TIME IN FOREVER

from FROZEN

Music and Lyrics by KRISTEN ANDERSON-LOPEZ
and ROBERT LOPEZ

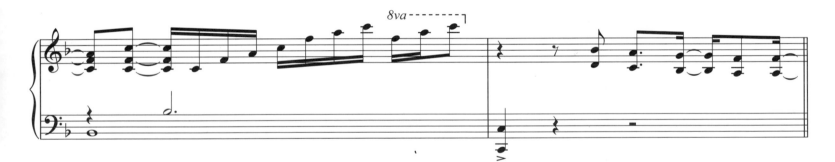

HOW DOES A MOMENT LAST FOREVER

from BEAUTY AND THE BEAST

Music by ALAN MENKEN
Lyrics by TIM RICE

Pedal ad lib. throughout

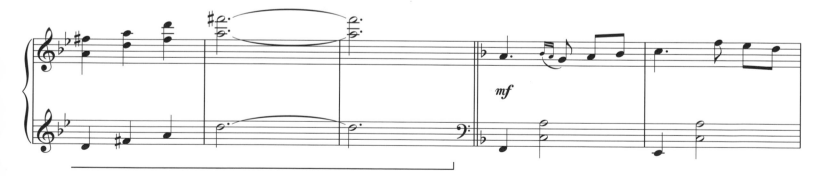

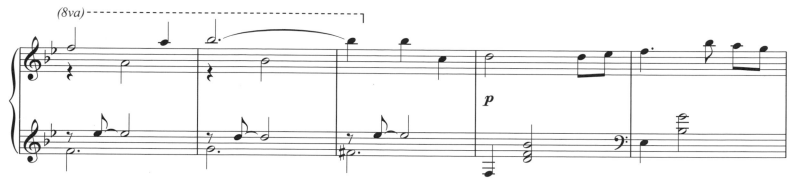

HOW FAR I'LL GO

from MOANA

Music and Lyrics by
LIN-MANUEL MIRANDA

Moderately

With pedal

I SEE THE LIGHT
from TANGLED

Music by ALAN MENKEN
Lyrics by GLENN SLATER

Moderately

With pedal

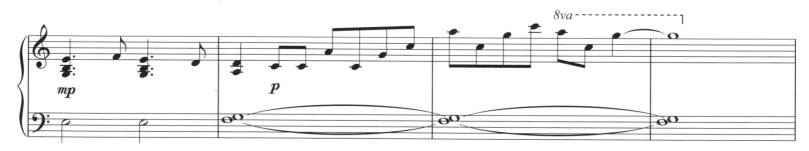

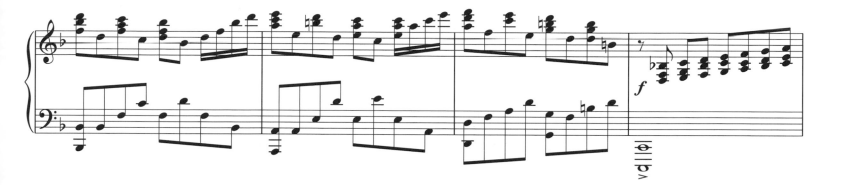

LET IT GO
from FROZEN

Music and Lyrics by KRISTEN ANDERSON-LOPEZ
and ROBERT LOPEZ

Steadily, with drive

A WHOLE NEW WORLD

(Aladdin's Theme)
from ALADDIN

Music by ALAN MENKEN
Lyrics by TIM RICE

Gospel Funk

MICKEY MOUSE MARCH

from THE MICKEY MOUSE CLUB

Words and Music by
JIMMIE DODD

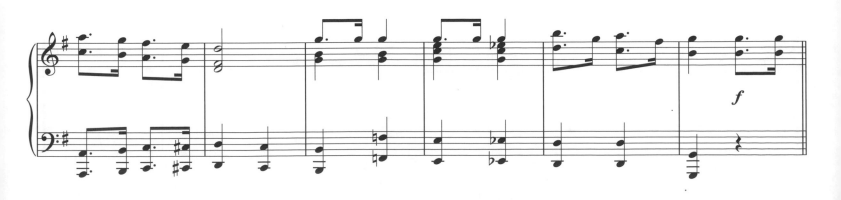

REMEMBER ME
(Ernesto de la Cruz)
from COCO

Words and Music by KRISTEN ANDERSON-LOPEZ
and ROBERT LOPEZ

Moderate Waltz

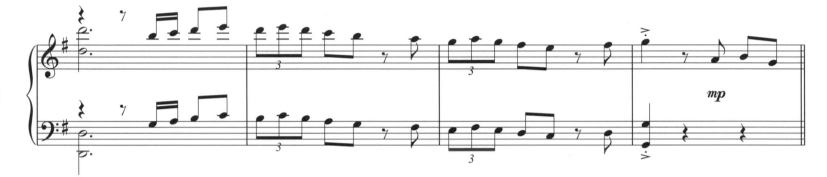

Bombastic

ff

Pedal ad lib.

mp sub.

WHEN SHE LOVED ME
from TOY STORY 2

Music and Lyrics by
RANDY NEWMAN

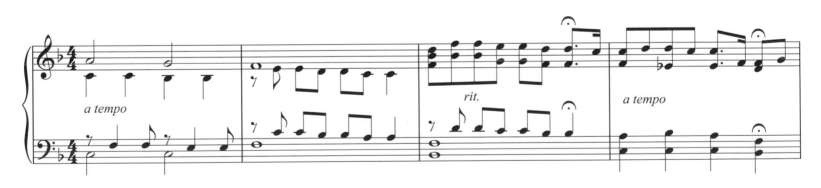

A little slower   **Freely**

Slower

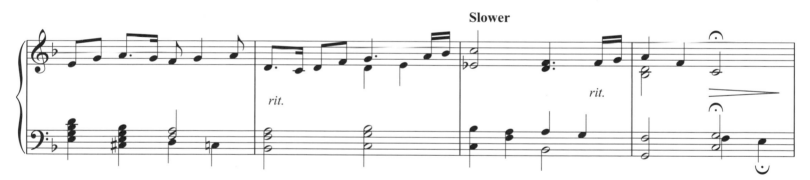

Tempo I

Very slowly

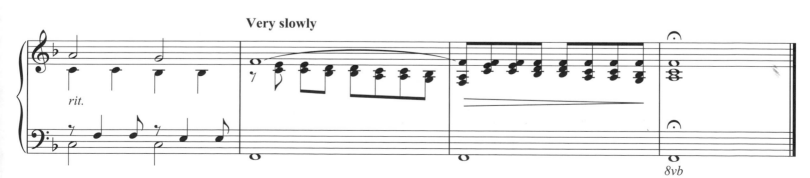

8vb

YOU'LL BE IN MY HEART

(Pop Version)*
from TARZAN®

Words and Music by
PHIL COLLINS

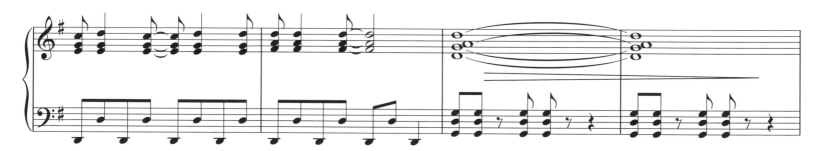

YOU'RE WELCOME
from MOANA

Music and Lyrics by
LIN-MANUEL MIRANDA

Moderately fast

YOU'VE GOT A FRIEND IN ME

from TOY STORY

Music and Lyrics by
RANDY NEWMAN

Gentle Swing

ZIP-A-DEE-DOO-DAH
from SONG OF THE SOUTH

Music by ALLIE WRUBEL
Words by RAY GILBERT

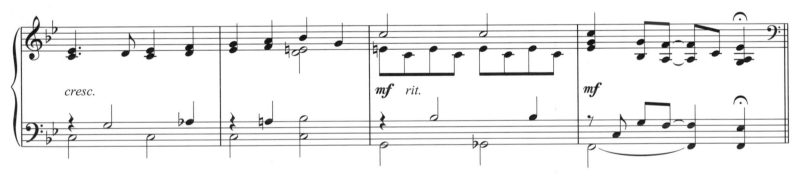

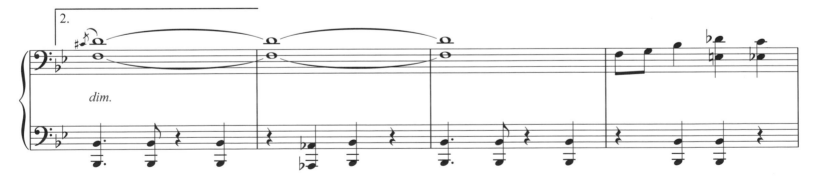

Creative PIANO SOLO

Looking to add some variety to your playing? Enjoy these beautifully distinctive arrangements for piano solo! These popular tunes get new and unique treatments for a fun and fresh presentation. Explore new styles and enjoy these favorites with a bit of a twist! Each collection includes 20 songs for the intermediate to advanced player.

BOHEMIAN RHAPSODY & OTHER EPIC SONGS

Band on the Run • A Day in the Life • Free Bird • November Rain • Piano Man • Roundabout • Stairway to Heaven • Take the Long Way Home • and more.

00196019 Piano Solo..$14.99

CHRISTMAS CAROLS

Away in a Manger • Deck the Hall • The First Noel • God Rest Ye Merry, Gentlemen • Hark! the Herald Angels Sing • It Came upon the Midnight Clear • Jingle Bells • Joy to the World • O Holy Night • Silent Night • Up on the Housetop • We Three Kings of Orient Are • What Child Is This? • and more.

00147214 Piano Solo..$14.99

CHRISTMAS COLLECTION

Blue Christmas • The Christmas Song (Chestnuts Roasting on an Open Fire) • Frosty the Snow Man • Here Comes Santa Claus (Right down Santa Claus Lane) • Let It Snow! Let It Snow! Let It Snow! • Silver Bells • Sleigh Ride • White Christmas • Winter Wonderland • and more.

00172042 Piano Solo..$14.99

CLASSIC ROCK

Another One Bites the Dust • Aqualung • Beast of Burden • Born to Be Wild • Carry on Wayward Son • Layla • Owner of a Lonely Heart • Roxanne • Smoke on the Water • Sweet Emotion • Takin' It to the Streets • 25 or 6 to 4 • Welcome to the Jungle • and more!

00138517 Piano Solo..$14.99

Prices, contents, and availability subject to change without notice.

DISNEY FAVORITES

Beauty and the Beast • Can You Feel the Love Tonight • Chim Chim Cher-ee • For the First Time in Forever • How Far I'll Go • Let It Go • Mickey Mouse March • Remember Me (Ernesto de la Cruz) • You'll Be in My Heart • You've Got a Friend in Me • and more.

00283318 Piano Solo..$14.99

JAZZ POP SONGS

Don't Know Why • I Just Called to Say I Love You • I Put a Spell on You • Just the Way You Are • Killing Me Softly with His Song • Mack the Knife • Michelle • Smooth Operator • Sunny • Take Five • What a Wonderful World • and more.

00195426 Piano Solo..$14.99

JAZZ STANDARDS

All the Things You Are • Beyond the Sea • Georgia on My Mind • In the Wee Small Hours of the Morning • The Lady Is a Tramp • Like Someone in Love • A Nightingale Sang in Berkeley Square • Someone to Watch Over Me • That's All • What'll I Do? • and more.

00283317 Piano Solo..$14.99

POP BALLADS

Against All Odds (Take a Look at Me Now) • Bridge over Troubled Water • Fields of Gold • Hello • I Want to Know What Love Is • Imagine • In Your Eyes • Let It Be • She's Got a Way • Total Eclipse of the Heart • You Are So Beautiful • Your Song • and more.

00195425 Piano Solo..$14.99

POP HITS

Billie Jean • Fields of Gold • Get Lucky • Happy • Ho Hey • I'm Yours • Just the Way You Are • Let It Go • Poker Face • Radioactive • Roar • Rolling in the Deep • Royals • Smells like Teen Spirit • Viva la Vida • Wonderwall • and more.

00138156 Piano Solo..$14.99

HAL•LEONARD®

www.halleonard.com